Simple Prayers for Women

by
Kenneth and Karen Boa

Honor Books
Tulsa, Oklahoma

Unless otherwise indicated, all Scripture passages are paraphrased by the authors.

Simple Prayers for Women
ISBN 1-56292-601-2
Copyright © 1999 by Kenneth and Karen Boa
One Piedmont Center, Suite 130
Atlanta, Georgia 30305-1501

Published by Honor Books
P.O. Box 55388
Tulsa, Oklahoma 74155

INTRODUCTION

The concept of communicating with God—talking with Him just as we would talk with an intimate friend—is one of the great experiences of the Christian life. You, too, can have such a personal relationship with God by being diligent to converse with Him in prayer and listen to His voice in Scripture.

Simple Prayers for Women was designed to provide both the form and freedom needed to experience true communication with God. Form is present through Scripture and freedom comes as you respond to Scripture through your own thoughts and prayers. Together they represent a means by which you can take communication with God from concept to reality.

We pray that you will grow and flourish as you follow this path to the heart of God.

Blessings,

Kenneth and Karen Boa

*Many, O Lord my God, are the wonders
You have done, and Your thoughts toward us no one
can recount to You; were I to speak and tell of them,
they would be too many to declare.*

PSALM 40:5

Lord, I thank You for Your beloved Son,
for Your unfailing love, and for Your wonderful
thoughts. During my busy day, help me to remember
all that You have done for me. Help me to follow
Your Word and walk in purity of heart.

I have been loved by God and called to be a saint;
grace and peace have been given to me from
God our Father and the Lord Jesus Christ.

R O M A N S 1 : 7

Lord, You are intimately acquainted with
my ways. You love me and always have my best
interests at heart. I thank You for Your power, for
Your patience, and for Your compassion. I ask You
to help me walk as a Godly woman in the path
of love with You and with others.

*You have given us a new commandment to love
one another even as You have loved us; so we must love
one another. By this all men will know that we are
Your disciples, if we have love for one another.*

JOHN 13:34-35

Lord, I am awed by Your majesty and
humbled by Your infinite love for me. I thank
You that You will perfect me in Christ Jesus, so
I may demonstrate Your mercy and love to others.
I ask You to help me extend Your love to my
family, my friends, and to all those I meet today.

*He who sows sparingly will also reap sparingly,
and he who sows bountifully will also reap bountifully.*

2 CORINTHIANS 9:6

Lord, I thank You for Your tender mercies
and faithfulness and for the greatness of Your name.
I thank You for Your Son, Jesus Christ, Who has
sown light into my life. Teach me to sow bountifully
by being generous to others and giving of myself to
my family and all those who cross my path.

As for me and my household, we will serve the Lord.

JOSHUA 24:15

Lord, I want Your Word to be deeply implanted in me so that I will know the truth and be able to express it in the way I live. I want my children to learn about You, not only from my words but from my daily walk with You. Help me to develop strength, patience, and a loving nature. Let my children see that their mother is devoted to knowing and following You.

*I will give thanks to the Lord, call upon His
name, and make known to others what He has done.
I will sing to Him, sing praises to Him, and tell of all
His wonderful acts.*

1 C HRONICLES 16:8-9

Lord, my lips are filled with praise for Your awesome deeds of righteousness. I thank You for Your wonderful acts, and I ask that You would increase my eagerness to respond to Your Word. Teach me to be more thankful for all Your blessings, especially the blessing of being a woman.

*Like Abraham, I should direct my children
and my household after me to keep the way of
the Lord by doing what is right and just.*

GENESIS 18:19

Lord, the earth proclaims Your splendor and majesty, and my heart rejoices for every word that proceeds from Your mouth. I thank You for delivering my soul from the depths of the grave. From this day forth, I will obey Your commandments to teach, nurture, and serve those in my family.

Lord, You have said, "Come to Me, all you who labor and are heavy laden, and I will give you rest. Take My yoke upon you and learn from Me, for I am gentle and humble in heart, and you will find rest for your souls. For My yoke is easy, and My burden is light."

MATTHEW 11:28-30

Lord, how greatly I need Your rest.
When I feel tired and stressed from the burdens
of life, help me to remember that You are always with
me and the Comforter Himself indwells my heart.
Search me and know me, for You are my God.

The integrity of the upright guides them,
but the unfaithful are destroyed by their duplicity.

PROVERBS 11:3

Lord, my own goodness fails me, but by the blood of Christ, I have become righteous in Your sight. I thank You that You have blessed me with every spiritual blessing. Help me to walk in integrity and shine as a light on a hill, pointing others to You.

I was once darkness, but now I am light in the Lord.
May I walk as a child of light (for the fruit of the light
consists in all goodness and righteousness and truth),
learning what is pleasing to the Lord.

EPHESIANS 5:8-10

Lord, as I approach Your throne of grace today,
I am grateful that You care about the things that
concern me. I thank You for seating me at Your right
hand in Christ, and I am determined to set my heart
on heavenly things. Teach me how to be Your
daughter and always walk in Your light.

Reckless words pierce like a sword,
but the tongue of the wise brings healing.

PROVERBS 12:18

Lord, teach me to speak words that will build others up rather than tear them down. Place a guard over my mouth that I may not destroy the faith or confidence of others. Give me wisdom and help me to think before I speak. Fill me each day with Your Spirit that I might enrich the lives of others.

Peace You leave with me; Your peace You give to me.
Not as the world gives, do You give to me.
I will not let my heart be troubled nor let it be fearful.

JOHN 14:27

Lord, I thank You for Your glorious works
and for Christ, my Redeemer. I thank You for
the peace Jesus gives me, as I remember He spoke
"Peace!" to the waves and they were stilled.
Help me to continually abide in Your peace,
even during the storms in my life.

I will not judge, so that I will not be judged.
For in the same way I judge others, I will be judged;
and with the measure I use, it will be measured to me.

MATTHEW 7:1-2

Lord, I look to You as my example of love
and compassion. Give me a humble heart that
responds to Your rebuke, and teach me to judge
myself rather than others. Then will I know
that I am truly Your child.

*I will not lay up for myself treasures on earth,
where moth and rust destroy and where thieves break
in and steal. But I will lay up for myself treasures in
heaven, where moth and rust do not destroy and where
thieves do not break in and steal. For where my
treasure is, there my heart will be also.*

MATTHEW 6:19-21

Lord, You rule righteously over us and Your Son, Jesus, came in humility as a servant. Teach me to be a servant as well. Help me to lay up spiritual treasures; for where my treasure is, there my heart will be also.

I will not worry about tomorrow, for tomorrow will worry about itself. Each day has enough trouble of its own.

MATTHEW 6:34

Lord, Your wonderful works are gifts
to Your children. I thank You that I can find
comfort through hope in You. I will not worry
about worldly things but will remember Your many
blessings and promises to me. Help me not to worry
about those things which may never happen,
but rather to place my trust in You.

I will not withhold good from those to whom it is due,
when it is in my power to act.

PROVERBS 3:27

Lord, I thank You that You rise to show compassion and reward me for my commitment to Christ. Help me to be just and kind to others. Help me to remember the poor and needy, not only in my prayers but in my deeds. Show me what I can do to help those You have called me to serve.

*Godliness with contentment is great gain.
For I brought nothing into the world, and I can
take nothing out of it. But if I have food and
clothing, with these I will be content.*

1 TIMOTHY 6:6-8

Lord, Your goodness flows over me like warm
sunshine as I rejoice in the revelation of Your Son.
I thank You for the hope of my resurrection.
I purpose in my heart to be thankful for all You
give me. Teach me to be content wherever I am,
knowing You will always meet my needs.

*I will contribute to the needs
of the saints and practice hospitality.*

ROMANS 12:13

Lord, Your judgments are true and righteous
and You give life to all things. I delight in Your Word
and dedicate myself to serve the needs of others as
You lead me. Help me to create a home where my
family feels loved and others feel welcome.

Starting a quarrel is like breaching a dam,
so I will stop a quarrel before it breaks out.

PROVERBS 17:14

Lord, I thank You for Your sovereign
power and for Your promise of complete renewal.
I thank You for the many things You have given me.
Help me to be self-controlled and live in peace
with others. Put a guard on my lips so that
I may only speak words of life.

*Thanks be to God, who gives us the victory through
our Lord Jesus Christ. Therefore, I will be steadfast,
immovable, abounding in the work of the Lord,
knowing that my labor in the Lord is not in vain.*

1 CORINTHIANS 15:57-58

Lord, You are worthy of all praise and Jesus is
the source of eternal salvation for all who obey Him.
I thank You for the peace and hope I enjoy in Him,
and I ask that I would abound in the work of the
Lord and hold firmly to the truth without wavering.

I will train up each child according to His way;
even when he is old, he will not depart from it.

PROVERBS 22:6

Lord, I thank You that You are clothed
with majesty and that Jesus came to set me free.
I thank You for Your gift of eternal life through faith
in Christ. Guide me as I instruct my children in the
ways of righteousness and truth. Let me always
remember that I am only a steward of their gifts and
talents as they grow in the knowledge of You.

*In Christ Jesus, God's whole building is joined
together and growing into a holy temple in the Lord;
in Whom we also are being built together
into a dwelling of God in the Spirit.*

EPHESIANS 2:21-22

Lord, I worship You as the eternal King
and marvel at the gift of Your grace in Christ Jesus
abounded to the many. Help me to edify others for
Your glory, building them up in faith. Teach me to
lay a firm foundation in Christ within my own
spirit so that I might help others.

*There are different kinds of gifts, but the
same Spirit. And there are different kinds of service,
but the same Lord. And there are different kinds of
working, but the same God works all of them in all
people. But to each one, the manifestation of the
Spirit is given for the common good.*

1 CORINTHIANS 12:4-7

Lord, I bow my head in worship as I consider Your wisdom and power. I thank You for being my stronghold and my refuge. Teach me to see Your Spirit working in others. Help me to recognize and exercise my God-given gifts in the service of others.

There should be no division in the body,
but its members should have the same concern for
each other. If one member suffers, all the members
suffer with it; if one member is honored, all the
members rejoice with it. Now we are the body of Christ,
and each one of us is a member of it.

1 CORINTHIANS 12:25-27

Lord, I thank You for Your wondrous power
and for the greatness of Your salvation in Jesus.
I thank You for instructing and teaching me in the
way I should go, and I ask that You would put within
me a deeper concern for the welfare and unity
of the body of Christ. I resolve to remember the
martyred church in other countries and to pray
for those in the body who are persecuted.

We must encourage one another daily,
as long as it is still called "Today," lest any of
us be hardened by the deceitfulness of sin.

HEBREWS 3:13

Lord, Your ways are limitless, and You feed
Your flock like a shepherd. I thank You for working
all things together for my highest good. Help me to be
a source of encouragement to others and a woman
whose ways are pleasing to You.

The harvest is plentiful, but the workers are few.
Therefore, I will pray that the Lord of the
harvest will send out workers into His harvest field.

MATTHEW 9:37-38; LUKE 10:2

Lord, You reign over all things and hold the earth in
the palm of Your hand. I thank You that You give
grace and glory, and I ask that I would be privileged
to participate in Your harvest. I pray that I would use
every opportunity, whether in person, by telephone,
or in a letter, to be a witness of Your gift of salvation.

I want everything I do to be done in love.

1 CORINTHIANS 16:14

Lord, I declare that Your Word never returns empty
and that You have set my heart on eternal things.
I am so honored that You have given me Your Holy
Spirit and made me the woman that I am. Because
Your love has been shed abroad in my heart, I choose
to walk in love and faithfulness every day of my life.

Teach me to number my days,
that I may gain a heart of wisdom.

P SALM 90:12

Lord, You are the Master of the heavens and the earth. I thank You for Your mercy and faithfulness. Help me to recognize the brevity of my earthly journey and live in wisdom and truth, setting an example for those in my household.

If I forgive men for their transgressions,
my heavenly Father will also forgive me.

M A T T H E W   6 : 1 4

Lord, I stand in awe of Your eternal plan
and the heavens and the earth You have created.
I thank You that the Holy Spirit lives in me. I will
strive to love and forgive others just as I have been
loved and forgiven by You. Help me to be merciful, to
love those who do not love me, and to demonstrate
Your work of forgiveness in my life.

You are the light of the world. He who follows You will not walk in the darkness but will have the light of life.

JOHN 8:12

Lord, I thank You for the glory and majesty
of Jesus Christ and for the gift of forgiveness through
His death and resurrection. I thank You that You
light my path so that my steps will not falter. Help
me to be a woman of integrity, keeping Your
precepts always before me.

I will proclaim the name of the Lord
and praise the greatness of my God.

D E U T E R O N O M Y   3 2 : 3

Lord, Your power is great, and You are able to
do immeasurably more than all that I ask or think.
I thank You for calling me to worship You in spirit
and truth. Help me to be virtuous in my relationships
with others, giving honor to You in all things.
I choose to abide in Jesus Christ and walk in
prudence and the fear of the Lord.

I will not let any corrupt word come out of my mouth
but only what is helpful for building others up according
to their needs that it may impart grace to those who hear.

EPHESIANS 4:29

Lord, I rejoice to know that through my faith in Christ Jesus I may approach You with boldness and confidence. Help me always to speak words to others that portray humility and grace. I will boast only of Your lovingkindness, justice, and righteousness.

Whoever exalts himself will be humbled,
and whoever humbles himself will be exalted.

MATTHEW 23:12;

LUKE 14:11; 18:14

Lord, I thank You for strengthening those whose hearts are committed to You. Help me to be a good and faithful servant, as I humble myself before You. I acknowledge that all good and perfect things come from You, for You are my provider.

*I want to walk in a way that is worthy
of the calling with which I was called, with all
humility and meekness and patience.*

EPHESIANS 4:1-2

Lord, I praise You for Your righteousness
and for Your promise to make righteousness spring
up before all nations. I thank You that I was bought
at a price. Help me to walk in a way that is worthy
of the calling You have placed on my life.

We ought always to thank God for other believers and pray that their faith would grow more and more, and that the love each of them has toward one another would increase.

2 THESSALONIANS 1:3

Lord, You are worthy of all honor and praise.
I thank You for manifesting Yourself to those who
love You and for the people You place in my life.
I commit to pray for them on a regular basis, that
their faith in You would grow more and more.

The way of a fool is right in his own eyes,
but a wise man listens to counsel.

P R O V E R B S   1 2 : 1 5

Lord, I thank You that Christ is a servant to
those in need and is ever interceding for us. I now
present my body as a slave to righteousness, and I
choose to be wise in heart and listen to counsel. As
I learn to listen, teach me also to obey that I might
always walk confidently in Your presence.

I do not want to be worried and troubled
about many things; only one thing is needed.
Like Mary, I want to choose the good part,
which will not be taken away from me.

LUKE 10:41-42

Lord, Your love has been poured out
into my heart through the Holy Spirit. I will not
be anxious like Martha, but will choose the good part
as Mary did and focus my attention on You. Teach me
to sit at the feet of Jesus so that I may develop
a deeper relationship with Him.

*I have hidden Your Word in my heart
that I might not sin against You.*

PSALM 119:11

Lord, Your blessings are great and I rest
safely in Your tender care. Hide Your Word in
my heart, and keep my feet from every evil path.
Give me a discerning heart that is quick to hear
You and hands that are quick to obey.

*I will not forget to show hospitality to strangers, for by
so doing some have entertained angels without knowing it.*

H E B R E W S   1 3 : 2

Lord, I thank You that Jesus came
from heaven and that You gave all things unto
His hands. I thank You that I am saved through faith
in His precious name. Bless my efforts as I reach out
to those around me and tell them about Your love
and faithfulness. Strengthen my hands as
I strive to walk in Your footsteps.

*Because of our ministry of supplying
the needs of the saints, they will glorify God for
the obedience that accompanies our confession of the
gospel of Christ, and for the liberality of sharing
with them and with everyone else.*

2 CORINTHIANS 9:12-13

Lord, I praise You for Your awesome power
and for raising Jesus from the dead. I thank You
for choosing me in Christ before the foundation of
the world to be Your own dear child. Give me the
ability, knowledge, and willingness to assist
those around me who are in need.

Let him who thinks he stands take heed lest he fall.

1 CORINTHIANS 10:12

Lord, I thank You that You have revealed
Your majesty and glory to all people. I thank You
for Your salvation and deliverance. I will not hide
anger and enmity in my heart. I will speak the
truth to others in love and seek reconciliation.

I will trust in You enough to honor
You as holy in the sight of others.

NUMBERS 20:12

Lord, Your words are true, and You
credit righteousness to those who trust in You.
Guide me back to You when I fall into disobedience,
and teach me how to examine my ways. You have said
in Your Word that obedience is better than sacrifice.
Help me to know the difference.

*God comforts us in all our afflictions, so that
we can comfort those in any affliction with the comfort
we ourselves have received from God.*

2   C O R I N T H I A N S   1 : 4

Lord, I believe that You will reward
each person according to his works. Thank You for
turning my darkness into light and for comforting me
in my afflictions so that I may comfort and encourage
others. Set Your Word always before me so that I
might remember Your great and awesome deeds.
You are a faithful and just Father.

*I will do all things without complaining or
arguing, so that I may become blameless and pure,
a child of God without fault in the midst of a crooked
and perverse generation, among whom I shine as a
light in the world, holding fast the Word of life.*

PHILIPPIANS 2:14-16

Lord, I thank You for Your goodness
and everlasting love and for Jesus' desire for us
to be with Him and behold His glory. I know that
You send Your discipline for my good. I will pursue
purity in my character continuously so that I
may be an example to others in my world.

*I will seek first Your kingdom and
Your righteousness; and all these things shall be
added to me. Therefore, I will not be anxious for
tomorrow; for tomorrow will care for itself.*

MATTHEW 6:33-34

Lord, Your lovingkindness and truth
bring life to my body and soul. I thank You
for strengthening and upholding me. I will seek
Your righteousness and Your kingdom above all
things, for it is only in You that I find rest and
peace for myself and my household.

*I must not test the Lord or grumble
as some of the Israelites did.*

1 CORINTHIANS 10:9-10

Lord, I thank You for Your hand of justice and
for the priceless gift of eternal life in Christ. I thank
You that in Christ Jesus I cannot be condemned.
Help me not to grumble about my circumstances but
strive to be full of the Holy Spirit and faith, knowing
that You always have my best interests at heart.

Whatever I do, whether in word or in deed,
I will do all in the name of the Lord Jesus, giving
thanks to God the Father through Him.

C O L O S S I A N S   3 : 1 7

Lord, I dwell securely in the riches of
Your kindness, forbearance, and patience. I will
walk in Your ways by loving and serving You, sowing
to please the Spirit, and doing all things in the name
of Jesus Christ. Direct and guide my steps so that
I fulfill the desires of Your heart.

As we have opportunity, we should do good to all people, especially to those who belong to the family of faith.

GALATIANS 6:10

Lord, I desire to know the depth of Your
wisdom and knowledge so that I may approve
what is excellent and be sincere and blameless
before You. I pray that my love and knowledge of
You would abound as I minister to the saints.
Help me to recognize opportunities to serve
others at work, at church, and at home.

*I will obey those who lead me and submit
to them, for they keep watch over my soul as those
who must give an account. I will obey them, so that
they may do this with joy and not with grief,
for this would be unprofitable for me.*

HEBREWS 13:17

Lord, You are most worthy of praise and
rich in mercy and grace. I will submit to my spiritual
leaders and pray with joy for other believers that love
may abound in them. Help me to be sensitive toward
my spiritual leaders so that I may speak words
of encouragement rather than criticism.

Whatever is true, whatever is noble,
whatever is right, whatever is pure, whatever is lovely,
whatever is of good report—if anything is excellent or
praiseworthy—I will think about such things.
The things I have learned and received and heard and
seen in those who walk with Christ, I will practice,
and the God of peace will be with me.

PHILIPPIANS 4:8-9

Lord, Jesus has shown us Who You are
and given us the gift of the Holy Spirit. Help me to
set my mind on the things that are true, noble, right,
pure, lovely, and praiseworthy. But never let me
turn a blind eye to evil done to another. Give me
a courageous and willing heart to help others.

I will sanctify Christ as Lord in my heart,
always being ready to make a defense to everyone
who asks me to give the reason for the hope
that is in me, but with gentleness and respect.

1 PETER 3:15

Lord, help me to comprehend the surpassing greatness of knowing You, and how to use wisdom, tactfulness, and clarity when I tell others about You. Help me to love others as You love them and always respond with a gentle spirit when I am questioned about the One Who dwells within me.

*If I do not judge, I will not be judged; if I do not condemn,
I will not be condemned; if I forgive, I will be forgiven.*

LUKE 6:37

Lord, Your forgiveness is the sure and unchanging foundation of my faith. I thank You that You have made it available to me through my faith in Your Son. Teach me to forgive others as I have been forgiven—not to judge others, but to love them with brotherly love and honor them above myself.

As an alien and a stranger in the world, I will abstain from fleshly lusts, which war against my soul.

1 PETER 2:11

Lord, I thank You for Your compassion for the
afflicted and the poor and the way in which Your
Son demonstrated that compassion. I thank You that
He is the Living Bread that came down from heaven.
Help me to live as an honorable woman by abstaining
from those things that are displeasing to You.

By this we know love, that Christ laid down His life for us, and we ought to lay down our lives for the brethren.

1 JOHN 3:16

Lord, my heart is humbled by Your holiness and Your mighty deeds. Your kindness and faithfulness overwhelm me. Teach me to love others in the same way You have loved me. Open my heart to see those around me who need to feel Your love and hear Your words of comfort and encouragement.

The tongue that brings healing is a tree of life,
but perverseness in it crushes the spirit.

P R O V E R B S   1 5 : 4

Lord, I know that You take no pleasure
in wickedness and that Your mercy and grace are
sufficient to forgive even the most grievous wrongs.
I thank You for pouring out Your forgiveness on
me as I turn from evil and walk in Your ways.
Teach me to edify others in the things I say
and build them up in faith.

I will put away all of these things: anger, wrath, malice, slander, and abusive language from my mouth.

COLOSSIANS 3:8

Lord, I thank You for Your desire that
the wicked would turn from their ways and live.
I thank You for Your power that is made perfect
in my weakness. Keep me from anger, and
teach me to choose my words wisely.

The foremost commandment is this: "Hear, O Israel, the Lord our God, the Lord is one; and you shall love the Lord your God with all your heart and with all your soul and with all your mind and with all your strength." The second is this: "You shall love your neighbor as yourself." There is no commandment greater than these.

MARK 12:29-31

Lord, Your judgments are always right and just.
I pray that as I consecrate myself and determine to
be holy, I will love You with all my heart, soul, mind,
and strength and love my neighbor as myself. Help
me to understand Your will more fully and give
me strength to walk in Your ways.

When pride comes, then comes dishonor,
but with humility comes wisdom.

P R O V E R B S   1 1 : 2

Lord, help me to guard myself from pride
and boasting that I might gain wisdom. Give me
the heart of a woman who is meek and gentle before
You. Search my heart and show me where I fall short
of Your standard of humility in all my interactions
with others; for I know that when I walk in pride,
my life is not pleasing to You.

Peter came to Jesus and asked, "Lord, how often shall my brother sin against me, and I forgive him? Up to seven times?" Jesus said to him, "I tell you, not seven times, but up to seventy times seven."

MATTHEW 18:21-22

Lord, I determine by an act of my will
not to justify myself before others. Help me to
forgive those who have injured me just as I have
been forgiven. I thank You for the unmeasureable
portion of mercy and grace that Christ provided
for me through His sacrifice on the cross.
Give me opportunities to follow His example.

Humility and the fear of the Lord
bring wealth and honor and life.

P R O V E R B S   2 2 : 4

Lord, I praise You for Your greatness and
trust in Your promise that nothing is impossible
for You. I will look to You for promotion rather than
striving to promote myself. Beginning today, I choose
not to be wise in my own eyes but to live in humility
and the fear of the Lord. I thank You for the
rest that I find in Your presence.

Blessed are the poor in spirit, for theirs is the kingdom of heaven. Blessed are those who mourn, for they will be comforted. Blessed are the meek, for they will inherit the earth.

MATTHEW 5:3-5

Lord, I thank You for Your matchless holiness
and for the glory of Your creation. Keep me ever
mindful of Your blessings and my complete
dependence on Your Son, Jesus Christ. Help me to
reach out in compassion to those who mourn.

The hour has come for me to wake up from sleep, for my salvation is nearer now than when I first believed. The night is nearly over; the day is almost here. Therefore I will cast off the works of darkness and put on the armor of light.

ROMANS 13:11-12

Lord, nothing shall escape Your perfect judgment, and the sufferings of this present time are not worthy to be compared with the glory that will be revealed to me through Your Spirit. Help me to walk in the light of Your truth and cast off the works of darkness, living as an example of godly womanhood.

As one who has believed in God, I want to be careful to devote myself to doing what is good. These things are good and profitable for everyone.

TITUS 3:8

Lord, I thank You that You do great things
which we cannot comprehend and that You speak
with crowning authority. I thank You that my hope
in Christ is the sure and steadfast anchor of my soul.
I will devote myself to becoming a woman who
goes about doing what is good.

I want to learn to be content in whatever circumstances
I am in. Whether I am abased or in abundance,
whether I am filled or hungry, I want to learn the secret
of being content in any and every situation.
I can do all things through Him who strengthens me.

PHILLIPIANS 4:11-13

Lord, I ask You to help me as I guard my
heart against covetousness. I determine to be
thankful for all that You have done for me, especially
the inheritance You have provided for all who
believe in Christ. Teach me to be content and give
thanks in all the circumstances of my life.

I will not let love and truth leave me; I will bind them around my neck and write them on the tablet of my heart.

PROVERBS 3:3

Lord, I thank You that You are the Great
Shepherd and I am part of Your flock. I cling to
Your promise that I cannot be separated from Your
love and truth no matter what storms blow through
my life. Help me speak anointed words as I tell others
about You and Your great gift for all mankind.

I will give generously to others without a grudging heart.

D E U T E R O N O M Y 1 5 : 1 0

Lord, I praise You for Your love, grace,
and Your fellowship. Keep me always mindful of all
I have been given and ready to be generous with the
resources You have entrusted to me. I look forward to
the opportunities You will provide for me to bless
others and myself through the gift of giving.

*As one who has been chosen of God,
holy and beloved, I will put on a heart of compassion,
kindness, humility, gentleness, and patience, bearing
with others and forgiving others even as the Lord forgave
me; and above all these things, I will put on love,
which is the bond of perfection.*

COLOSSIANS 3:12-14

Lord, I believe that You have chosen me for
Your purpose and made me Your child. I will put on
a heart of compassion, kindness, humility, gentleness,
patience, and most importantly, love. Help me to treat
others with the same compassion and kindness that
was poured out on me, loving as I have been loved
and forgiving as I have been forgiven.

Since I belong to the day, I will be self-controlled,
putting on the breastplate of faith and love,
and the hope of salvation as a helmet.

1 THESSALONIANS 5:8

Lord, I thank You for Your Son
who has revealed You and for the truth that
He could return for us at any time. I thank You
that my salvation is in repentance and rest. I will
walk in faith and love, knowing that my hope
and trust are firmly secured in You.

I will not be afraid of my adversaries, but I will remember the Lord, Who is great and awesome.

NEHEMIAH 4:14

Lord, I have placed my confidence in You
and rest in Your promise to fight my battles for me.
I will not be afraid, but I will set my heart on You
and place my trust in Your greatness. Help me as
I strive to overcome evil with good.

*I will rejoice in hope, persevere in affliction,
and continue steadfastly in prayer.*

ROMANS 12:12

Lord, I place my hope in You that You do not change
and that You alone do wonderful things. Help me
as I encounter affliction to trust You and persevere
in the light of eternity. I ask that You will strengthen
me and help me to become a woman of prayer.

We who are strong ought to bear the weaknesses of those who are not strong, and not to please ourselves. Each of us should please his neighbor for his good, to build him up.

ROMANS 15:1-2

Lord, the whole family in heaven and earth
derives its name from You. I thank You for the
sisters and brothers You have given me in Christ.
Help me to walk in love by considering their
needs and interests above my own.

*I am hard pressed on every side, but not crushed;
perplexed, but not in despair; persecuted, but not forsaken;
struck down, but not destroyed; always carrying about in
my body the death of Jesus, so that the life of Jesus may
also be revealed in my body. For we who live are always
being delivered over to death for Jesus' sake, so that
His life may be revealed in our mortal body .*

2 CORINTHIANS 4:8-11

Lord, You are worthy of all glory and You have complete dominion over all things. I thank You for the love of Christ Who died for me. Give me courage as I encounter the storms of life and help me to remember that when I suffer, Your life is revealed in me.

I will guard my heart with all diligence,
for out of it flow the issues of life.

P R O V E R B S 4 : 2 3

Lord, I thank You for the glory of Your name
and for creating the heavens and earth through Your
power and wisdom. I thank You that godly sorrow
leads to repentance. I will guard my heart and be
strengthened in every good work and deed.

*I will fight the good fight, finish the race, and keep
the faith so that there will be laid up for me the crown of
righteousness, which the Lord, the righteous Judge, will
award to me on that day; and not only to me, but also
to all who have longed for His appearing.*

2 TIMOTHY 4:7-8

Lord, I magnify Your blessed and everlasting name.
I thank You for qualifying me to share an inheritance
in the kingdom of Your beloved Son. Help me to learn
endurance through my trials and finish my race well.

If I lack wisdom, I should ask of God,
Who gives generously to all without reproach,
and it will be given to me.

JAMES 1:5

Lord, I marvel at Your mighty acts and
Your forgiveness that has been given to me
through Christ. As I ask for Your wisdom,
help me to understand Your will for my life.
Guide me, teach me, and lead me into all truth.
Help me to be a strong and godly woman.

I will lay up Your words in my heart and in my soul and teach them to my children, talking about them when I sit in my house and when I walk along the way and when I lie down and when I rise up.

DEUTERONOMY 11:18-19

Lord, the covenant You made with Abraham
has brought blessing to all those who determine to
walk by faith. I thank You for leading and guiding
me. Help me to lay up Your words in my heart
and teach them to my children and to others.

ABOUT THE AUTHORS

Kenneth Boa is engaged in a ministry of relational evangelism, discipleship, teaching, writing, and speaking. He holds a B.S. from Case Institute of Technology, a Th.M. from Dallas Theological Seminary, a Ph.D. from New York University, and a D. Phil. from the University of Oxford in England.

Dr. Boa is the president of Reflections Ministries, an organization that seeks to provide safe places for people to consider the claims of Christ and help them mature and bear fruit in their relationship with Him. He is also president of Trinity House Publishers, a publishing company dedicated to the creation of tools that will help people manifest eternal values in a temporal arena by drawing them to intimacy with God and a better understanding of the culture in which they live.

Karen Boa has a B.A. in English from Montclair State University and has done graduate work at New York University in comparative literature. She continues to develop her interests in literature, film, music, and art; and she is an avid gardener.

The Boa's have a free monthly teaching letter called *Reflections*. If you would like to be on the mailing list, please call: (800) DRAW NEAR (372-9632).

Additional copies of this book and other publications
by Dr. Kenneth Boa, are available
from your local bookstore.

Seasons of Prayer, In Word and Image
Simple Prayers Daybook
Simple Prayers for Graduates

Honor Books
Tulsa, Oklahoma